A LANGUAGE LEARNING ADVENTURE

GOODBYE USA
Bonjour la France
Volume Two

Anne Elizabeth Bovaird
Illustrated by Pierre Ballouhey

BARRON'S

D1307494

Tom dreamed he was flying over Paris.

From way up high, he saw *L'Arc de Triomphe*. It looked like a giant star with streets for arms.

He saw *La Tour Eiffel*—a tall, pointed tower made of metal.

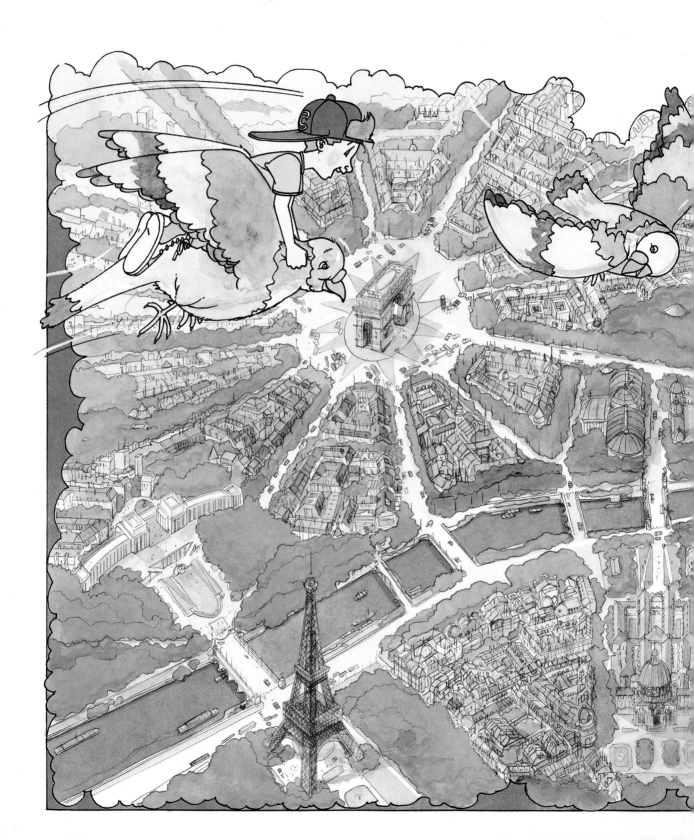

Then, Tom soared over *Le Louvre*, a famous old museum shaped like the letter U.

Next to *Le Louvre* is *La Place de la Concorde.* In the middle of *la Concorde* is a tall, stone column with Egyptian letters carved on it.

"*Bonjour Tom, ça va?*" called out a voice. He felt something wet on his cheek.

Tom sat up and rubbed his eyes. His cousin Pierre was leaning over one side of the bed tugging at the covers. *Médor*, his *chien*, was on the other side licking his face.

"Stop it, *Médor*. That tickles," said Tom. A little confused, he looked around the room. "Hey, where am I anyway?"

But Pierre just shrugged his shoulders. He didn't understand Tom because he doesn't speak any English.

"Now I remember. It wasn't a dream after all. I really am in Paris! *Bonjour Pierre. Bonjour Médor, ça va?*" shouted Tom, jumping out of bed. He ran to the window and looked out. In the street below, he saw people dressed up on their way to church.

"*C'est dimanche*," announced Pierre. He was glad to see his cousin finally awake.

"*C'est* D-mansh!" cried Tom. "I know, Pierre. You're saying it's Sunday. No school today!"

"I'm hungry. What's for breakfast?" Tom pointed to his stomach so his cousin would understand.

Pierre scratched his head. *"Le petit déjeuner?"*

"Oui Pierre, *le* pe-T day-juh-nay," repeated Tom. "That must mean breakfast!" Sometimes it was hard for Tom to talk to Pierre. There were so many words he didn't know in French. "Let's go eat. I'm starved!"

After Tom got dressed, the two boys went to the kitchen. *"Bonjour Maman, ça va?"* greeted Pierre. He gave his mother a kiss on both cheeks. *"Bonjour Papa, ça va?"* He kissed his father too.

"Bonjour Pierre. Ça va!" they answered.

Tom didn't like this French tradition of kissing too much so he simply said,

"*Bonjour Tante Nicole. Bonjour Oncle Jacques, ça va?* I'm hungry. Can I have some bacon and eggs and . . ."

"Slow down Tom," laughed *Tante Nicole*. "In France we don't eat that much for *le petit déjeuner*. *Petit* means 'little.' We eat a small breakfast."

"Why?" asked Tom. Luckily *Tante Nicole* and *Oncle Jacques* spoke English so they could explain these things to him.

"The French word for 'why' is *pourquoi*," his *tante* told him.

"Pour-quaw?" asked Tom, this time in French.

"*Parce que c'est comme ça.* Because that's the way it is. It's a French custom," she explained.

"Par-se-ke say come sa. Because it's like that in France," repeated Tom. But he really didn't understand. His mom always told him *le petit déjeuner* was the most important meal of the day.

For *le petit déjeuner*, Tom and Pierre are having:

des croissants
day craw-cen (t)

—rolls. Tom usually eats toast at home.

du beurre, de la confiture
du bur, duh la con-fee-tewr

—butter and jam.

du jus d'orange
du jew dO-ranj

—orange juice. Just like at home!

du chocolat chaud
du show-co-la show

—hot chocolate. Wait a minute. Hot chocolate in a bowl? Tom's mom would not be pleased if he drank from a bowl at the table!

Tante Nicole and *Oncle Jacques* are having:

du café	*du lait*	*du café au lait*
du ca-fay	du lay	
coffee	milk	coffee with milk.

Tom wanted to share some of his *petit déjeuner* with *Médor* who looked hungry. "Do we get more than one *croissant* for *le petit déjeuner, Tante Nicole?*" he asked.

"As many as you want," she said, sipping her *café au lait*. She handed Tom the basket of croissants. "*Ce sont des croissants. Ce sont* means 'these are,' because there's more than one."

"And," continued *Oncle Jacques*, "*C'est du jus d'orange. C'est* means 'this is,' because we're talking about only one thing."

Pierre helped himself to another *croissant* and dunked it in his *chocolat chaud*. Tom gave *Médor* a bite of *croissant* under the table.

During *le petit déjeuner*, Tom played a game with Pierre and his family. He made up sentences with *c'est* (THIS IS) and *ce sont* (THESE ARE).

Your turn! Look at the pictures and complete the sentences below with *c'est* or *ce sont* depending on whether it is plural or singular.

C_____ des croissants   C_____ du jus d'orange

C_____ Tom   C_____ des fleurs

C_____ un chien   C_____ deux cafés

C_____ une table   C_____ de la confiture

C_____ du beurre   C_____ deux chocolats chauds

C_____ du lait   C_____ dimanche

CE SONT DES CROISSANTS!

C'EST DU JUS D'ORANGE!

Eating all those *croissants* had made Pierre thirsty. "*Je voudrais du chocolat chaud, Maman,*" he asked.

"What does juh voo-dray mean?" Tom wanted to speak French as well as Pierre.

"It means 'I would like.' That's how you ask for things in French," explained *Oncle Jacques.*

"That's easy. *Je voudrais du chocolat chaud,*" bragged Tom holding up his bowl. He was trying hard to speak French.

"*S'il vous plaît,*" corrected Pierre.

"Oh, yeah. Please. I mean, *S'il vous plaît.* I was going to say it, you know."

After *le petit déjeuner, Tante Nicole* gave Pierre some money, a list, and a *caddie.* The ca-D looked like a basket on wheels.

"I'm sending you both to the market to buy food for *le déjeuner.*"

"*Le* day-juh-nay? *Qu'est-ce que c'est?*" asked Tom.

"That's lunch. On Sundays, we always eat a big lunch," replied *Tante Nicole*.

"*Pourquoi?*" demanded Tom.

"*Parce que c'est comme ça*. It's a tradition in France," she said.

Tom wasn't very satisfied with her answer. He still didn't understand why they ate a big *déjeuner* and a small *petit déjeuner*. And why did Pierre need a *caddie?* His parents always got bags at the supermarket back home! And shopping was for grown-ups, not kids. It was boring and Tom preferred to stay home and play.

"*Au revoir, Maman! Au revoir, Tante Nicole!*"

"*Au revoir, Tom! Au revoir, Pierre!*"

"*Ouaf, ouaf*," barked *Médor* in French.

"How much did your mom give you?" asked Tom when they were outside.

"*Combien?*" asked Pierre, trying to figure out what Tom was saying. "*Combien de francs?*"

"*Oui*, Pierre. Com-B-N. How many *francs* do you have?"

Pierre held out a fist full of change for Tom to count.

"*Un, deux, trois, quatre, cinq, six, sept, huit, neuf, dix francs*...I remember how to count to ten, but what about the rest? You have more than *dix francs!*"

Before they reached the market, Pierre taught Tom how to count to twenty. Practice saying the numbers below. Then help Pierre, Tom, and *Médor* find their way to the market by following the numbers!

onze	= 11 ownz	*quinze*	= 15 canz	*dix-huit*	= 18 deez-wheat
douze	= 12 dooz	*seize*	= 16 sez	*dix-neuf*	= 19 deez-nuhf
treize	= 13 trez	*dix-sept*	= 17 dee-set	*vingt*	= 20 van
quatorze	= 14 ca-torz				

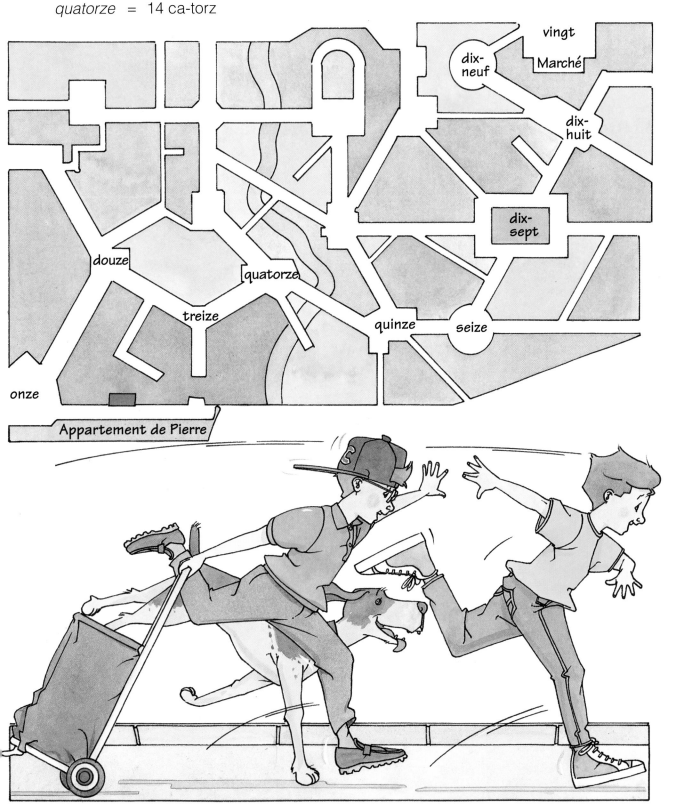

When they finally arrived at the market, Tom couldn't believe his eyes. "Hey, this isn't the grocery store!"

"*Non, Tom. C'est le marché*," said Pierre with a shrug.

"I like *le* mar-shay!" cried Tom looking around. "This is going to be fun!"

Instead of a giant indoor supermarket like they had at home, there were stalls lined up outside on the sidewalk. People were selling meat, fish, cheese, vegetables, fruit, and some things Tom didn't even recognize. Everything looked fresh and delicious!

Pierre walked up to one stall. On the counter, Tom saw all kinds of meat, chicken, and ducks.

"*Qu'est-ce que c'est?*" he asked.

"*C'est la boucherie.*" answered Pierre.

"*C'est la* boo-sherry. I know, this is the butcher's stall. But what are you going to buy?"

Pierre consulted his list. "*Un poulet,*" he said. He pointed to a chicken roasting on a spit. It smelled wonderful.

"*Un* poo-lay? I just hope it comes in a package!"

"*Bonjour Monsieur. Je voudrais un poulet, s'il vous plaît,*" said Pierre pointing to a whole chicken. "*C'est combien?*"

"*Vingt francs,*" answered the butcher. He picked out a chicken and put it in a bag.

"*Voilà, vingt francs,*" said Pierre, giving him 20 francs and putting the chicken in his *caddie.*

"*Merci, au revoir!*," he cried.

"*Au revoir!*," the butcher said.

Next, they went to a stall selling eggs, milk, and cheese.

Tom's nose didn't recognize all the varieties of cheeses on the shelves.

"*C'est la crémerie,*" announced Pierre.

"*La* cray-merry. Don't buy any of the cheese that smells really strong, Pierre!" groaned Tom. "*S'il vous plaît!*"

"*Bonjour Monsieur,*" said Pierre. *Je voudrais du fromage, s'il vous plaît.*" After he had selected some fro-maj, he asked, "*C'est combien?*"

"*Dix-sept francs,*" answered the man. Pierre handed him 17 francs.

"*Voilà dix-sept francs. Merci, au revoir!*"

"*Au revoir!,*" replied the man.

The two boys continued to walk through *le marché*. Pierre showed Tom a fish stall and said, "*C'est la poissonnerie*—pwa-so-nerry."

Luckily they didn't stop there because Tom didn't like the way those live crabs were looking at him.

After that, Pierre showed Tom a stall with all kinds of cold cuts and sausages. "*C'est la charcuterie*—shar-Q-terry."

Médor stuck his nose on the table to get a better look at the hot dogs.

Then they stopped at a fruit and vegetable stall. The man was shouting to shoppers to come buy his food.

"*Qu'est-ce que c'est?*"

"*C'est le marchand de fruits et légumes. Ce sont des fruits,*" said Pierre pointing to the fruit on one side of the counter. "*Ce sont des légumes.*" He pointed to the vegetables on the other side.

"*Le* mar-shan duh fruwe A lay-goom sells fruwe and lay-goom," repeated Tom. "Why does he have to yell so much? *Pourquoi?*"

"*Parce que c'est comme ça.*" answered Pierre.

Pierre bought lots of fruit from the vendor.

Match the French names and colors of the fruit with the English names and colors. Look at the numbers carefully! They will help you find the right answer!

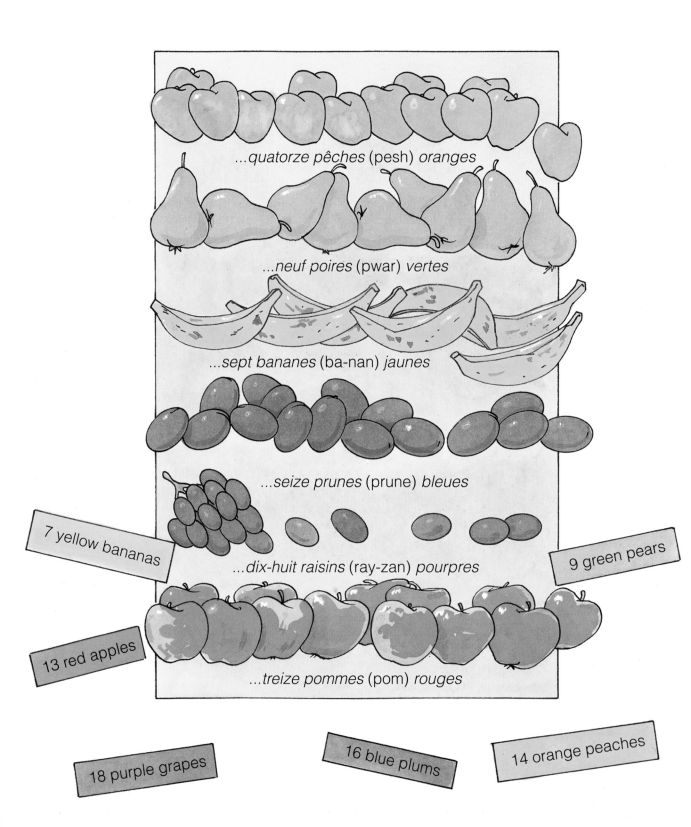

...*quatorze pêches* (pesh) *oranges*

...*neuf poires* (pwar) *vertes*

...*sept bananes* (ba-nan) *jaunes*

...*seize prunes* (prune) *bleues*

7 yellow bananas

9 green pears

...*dix-huit raisins* (ray-zan) *pourpres*

13 red apples

...*treize pommes* (pom) *rouges*

18 purple grapes

16 blue plums

14 orange peaches

Next, Pierre bought some green beans.

"*Bonjour Monsieur. Je voudrais un kilo de haricots verts, s'il vous plaît. C'est combien?*"

"*Dix-neuf francs*," said the man, weighing a bag of ar-E-co ver on a scale.

"Hey, I'm starting to understand how you buy things in French," said Tom excitedly.
"First you ask for something—*Je voudrais.*
Then you say how much is it—*C'est combien?*
Then you pay—*Voilà dix-neuf francs*
Then you say thank you—*Merci*
Then you say good-bye—*Au revoir!*

Can I try? Can I buy some of those tomatoes he's selling?"

But before Pierre could answer, Tom had already started talking.

"*Bonjour Monsieur,*" he said hesitantly. "*Je voudrais...des* toe-mat, *s'il vous plaît.* These, under here," said Tom, reaching for some big red tomatoes at the bottom of the pile. He started to pull one out when....

"*Non, Tom!*" screamed Pierre, waving his arms.

"*Ouaf! Ouaf!*" warned *Médor*, jumping up and down.

Too late. The pyramid of tomatoes came tumbling down.

"I'm really sorry! *Désolé, Monsieur!*" apologized Tom. He was very embarrassed. "I guess I should have let you choose for me."

The two boys quickly picked up the tomatoes. *Médor* helped by chasing the ones that had rolled under the table. Pierre was saying something to the man that Tom couldn't understand. He pointed to Tom and smiled quickly. Tom was glad Pierre was sticking up for him, but he knew he had done something wrong.

"*Au revoir Monsieur, merci!*" yelled Tom as Pierre dragged him away from *le marché*.

"Don't be mad Pierre," said Tom, after they left *le marché*. "I didn't mean to knock down all those tomatoes. Why can't we select our own, anyway? *Pourquoi?*"

"*PARCE QUE C'EST COMME CA!*" cried Pierre. He wished he could explain everything to Tom, but he didn't know how in English! He really liked his cousin but it was sometimes difficult to keep him out of trouble.

And Tom wished he could understand all these French customs. He thought about how easy it was to do things back home. And how easy it was to understand what people were saying.

Do you remember all the places they visited at *le marché*? Look at the list of food below and decide where you can buy:

crabe	*fromage*	*jambon*
haricots vertes	*poisson*	*bananes*
tomates	*concombre*	*saucisses*
poires	*raisin*	*poulet*
oeufs	*pêches*	*crevettes*
boeuf	*lait*	*carottes*

FRUITS ET LÉGUMES

LA CRÉMERIE

LA CHARCUTERIE

LA POISSONNERIE

LA BOUCHERIE

Before they reached the apartment, Pierre made a final stop in front of a bakery. "*C'est la boulangerie*," he said.

"*La* boo-lan-jerry," repeated Tom peeping in the window. He recognized some of the *croissants* they had for *le petit déjeuner*.

Inside, *la boulangerie* smelled great. Tom had never seen loaves of bread so long. And this bread was fresh and wasn't cut in slices and wrapped in plastic.

Pierre bought two long loaves of bread called *baguettes*.

Pierre handed Tom a *baguette*. It was still warm.

"*Une* ba-get for me? *Merci!*"

Pierre broke off two pieces. He gave one to *Médor* and popped the other into his mouth. Tom did the same.

"Pierre, this tastes great! You don't even need to put any *beurre* or *confiture* on it or anything!"

Pierre smiled at his cousin. He liked helping Tom discover new things about France.

On the way home, they pretended to be pirates and had a sword fight with their *baguettes.*

In the apartment, *Tante Nicole* took all the food and disappeared into the kitchen. At one o'clock, she finally called, "*À table*," which means, "Come and get it!" Tom was starved by then because his mom usually served lunch earlier.

For *le déjeuner*, they had all the things Pierre and Tom had bought at *le marché*. Look at *Tante Nicole's* shopping list and see if you can find each one of the foods.

After lunch, *Oncle Jacques* announced that they were going for a walk in *le Jardin du Luxembourg.*

"*Pourquoi?*" asked Tom.

"*Parce que, Tom,*" he replied. "A little bit of exercise helps us digest a big *déjeuner.*" Finally an answer to one of Tom's questions!

In *le Jardin du Luxembourg,* there was an old palace. There were footpaths and statues of famous French people everywhere. And there were *chaises* set up to sit down on.

It was a beautiful day and everyone was dressed up for an afternoon walk on *dimanche*.

Many children were playing in the gardens. Some had brought bikes, some were kicking soccer balls, and some were sitting in the sun.

"Oh, look! *C'est un chat!*" said Tom pointing to a cat playing with a butterfly. It made him think of his cat back home. "I hope she's not too lonely without me," he thought.

Tom started to walk across the grass when he heard a voice behind him shout, "*Non, Tom!*"

"What did I do wrong?" asked Tom, looking around.

"See that sign? It says *Pelouse interdite*. That means you aren't allowed to walk on the grass," explained *Oncle Jacques*. He pulled Tom back onto the path.

"Pe-loose an-ter-deet means you can't walk on the grass? *Pourquoi?*" asked Tom.

"*Parce que c'est comme ça.*"

"Another rule I don't understand," thought Tom.

"I'm not going to get into any more trouble," he told himself.

All of a sudden, he felt something biting his sleeve from behind the bushes. It had big teeth, a soft nose, and pointed ears. *Médor* started growling.

"*Qu'est-ce que c'est!*" cried Tom.

"*Ce sont des poneys!*" laughed Pierre. Sure enough, on the other side of the bushes Tom saw some ponies.

"*Des* po-nee!" repeated Tom with a sigh of relief. "In the middle of Paris?"

The children were taking turns riding *les poneys*. They all laughed and joked with each other. "I wish I knew what they were saying," thought Tom. "I'd like to laugh with them too."

One of the ponies walked up to Tom. "*Bonjour*," said Tom. "Do you speak English? My name is Tom." He reached into his pocket and pulled out an old candy bar. "Are you hungry?" Tom held out a piece for *le poney*.

Just then, he heard "*Non, Tom!*"

"You can't feed *les poneys*, Tom. It isn't allowed," explained *Tante Nicole*.

"*Pourquoi?*" asked Tom. "I wasn't hurting anything." He felt very embarrassed because everybody was looking at him.

"*Parce que c'est comme ça*," sighed his *tante*. "Come on, let's go see if we can find something else to do."

They went inside a small building at one end of *Le Jardin du Luxembourg*. "*Qu'est-ce que c'est?*" asked Tom excitedly, looking around when they were seated.

"*Ce sont des marionnettes*," explained Pierre, pointing to the stage.

"*Des* ma-ree-O-net?" repeated Tom. Just then the curtain went up. "Puppets!" he cried. "It's a puppet show!"

Les marionnettes were very funny. "Learning French is sometimes like watching a puppet show," Tom thought. "I can't always understand the words, but I can understand people's faces and the way they act."

Suddenly, Tom started to think about people he knew back home. "I wonder what my parents are doing now."

After the show, they went to a large fountain near the palace.

Children were sailing boats in it. They used big sticks to push them from one end to the other. Tom had never done that in Chicago!

"Look at those kids sailing boats! *Qu'est-ce que c'est* 'boat' in French?"

"A boat is *un bateau*," said *Oncle Jacques*.

"*Un* ba-toe," repeated Tom. "A boat. Boy, are they lucky! Can we sail *un bateau* too?"

Oncle Jacques gave Tom and Pierre each *douze francs*. They went up to the man renting the boats.

Tom is going to rent a boat. Do you remember how to ask for something in French?

Pierre and Tom took their boats to the fountain with the other children.

At the bottom of the fountain, Tom saw lots of French coins. "Why do people throw away their *francs* like that," he wondered. "If they don't want them anymore, I certainly do!"

Tom reached into the water and started to pick up some coins. Suddenly he heard "*NON, TOM!*" He turned around and saw Pierre shaking his head at him.

"*Pourquoi?*" he asked.

"*PARCE QUE C'EST COMME CA!*" Pierre cried impatiently.

Tom felt tears rising to his eyes. He was trying not to be upset, but he just couldn't help it. He was tired of doing everything wrong and being told no all the time.

"Everybody tells me what I can't do, but nobody explains why. I don't understand all the customs in France. I miss Chicago. I miss my mom and dad. I miss my *chat*. I miss talking to my friends. I want...*je voudrais*...I want to go home!" shouted Tom. With that, he started to cry.

Pierre was so startled he dropped his *bateau*. *Oncle Jacques* was so surprised he knocked over the *chaise* he was sitting on. *Médor* was so frightened he stuck his tail between his legs. *Tante Nicole* bent down and put her arms around Tom.

"Don't cry, Tom," said *Oncle Jacques*, handing him a handkerchief. "We don't want you to leave. I know Paris is not the same as Chicago and our customs are different from yours."

"And we forget how frustrating some things must be for you. You are right to ask all those questions, but sometimes it's hard to answer them," added *Tante Nicole*, giving Tom a big hug. "We're certainly going to try from now on."

"*Désolé, Tom*," added Pierre, patting Tom's back. He was sorry he got angry with Tom and made him cry.

Médor jumped up to lick Tom's face.

Tom sniffed a little. In fact, he really didn't want to leave. He liked Paris and seeing all the new places. And he liked Pierre. And he liked learning French, even though it was hard at times. He was just a little homesick.

"Well, OK. I'll stay."

"*Super, Tom!*" yelled Pierre, jumping up and down.

The two boys went back to sailing their boats. Tom laughed and played just like the other French children until it was time to go home.

For *le dîner*—D-nay, they had a light meal. And they ate later than Tom was used to—at 7:30.

"*Pourquoi*," asked Tom, "do you eat such a light dinner in France?"

"*Parce que*," explained *Oncle Jacques*. We had a big *déjeuner* and I haven't any room left for a big *dîner*!"

"Now that's logical!" shouted Tom. Everyone started to laugh at once.

For *le dessert*—day-ser, they had *du fromage, des pommes, du raisin,* and *des bananes*.

After dinner, Tom wrote a letter to his mom and dad about all the things he had done that Sunday.

Dear mom and dad,

Today is Sunday. Pierre told me it means dimanche in French. For le petit dejeuner, I had des croissants, du jus d'orange and du chocolat chaud. I even drank it from a bowl!

Then Pierre took me to le marché. You wouldn't believe it! All the stores were outside! Shopping isn't easy in France because you have go to lots of stalls to buy food. That's the custom. We went to la boulangerie, la crémerie and la boucherie.

Then Tante Nicole made a really big lunch with everything we bought. I don't really know pourquoi, Tante Nicole told me that in France, c'est comme ça. But it really doesn't matter. After that, we went to le Jardin du Luxembourg. There's lots of things to do there. You can ride les poneys and see les marionnettes. And there's a big fountain where kids can sail des bateaux. I rented one all by myself! I miss you. I felt a little homesick but I'm better now. I'm glad to be in France with Pierre, Tante Nicole and Oncle Jacques. I'll write soon!

Love,

Tom.

Guide to French Pronunciation

Pronouncing French isn't always easy! That's why Tom must repeat every French word he hears. Whenever possible, he uses English words that sound the same as the French word to help him speak French like Pierre. Here is the "secret code" that Tom uses for representing the correct sound in French.

• When you see a capital letter, pronounce it as if you were reciting the alphabet.
> Example: *viande*   V-and

• When you see a letter in parentheses, pronounce the word as you would in English, but omit the letter that is enclosed by the parentheses.
> Example: *Une*   (j)une

• Nasals are special sounds pronounced in some French words. You can recognize a nasal when you see a vowel (a, e, i, o, u) followed by an N or an M in Tom's pronunciation code.
> Example: *Chien*   she-N

Tom has a lot of trouble saying nasals correctly. He usually stops just short of pronouncing the N or the M. (These sounds are called nasals because the sound comes through your nose when you say them.)

Glossary (French—English)

French	Pronunciation	English
A		
*A table!**	a(t) ta(p)-bla	Come and get it!
Arc de Triomphe	ark duh tree-omph	Arch of Triumph
*Au revoir**	or-vwar	Good bye
B		
Baguette	ba-get	Type of French bread
Banane	ba-nan	Banana
Bateau	ba-toe	Boat
Beurre	bur	Butter
*Bonjour**	bon-joor	Good day
Boucherie	boo-sherry	Butcher's shop
Boulangerie	boo-lan-jerry	Bakery
Bleu	bluh	Blue
C		
*Ca va?**	sa(t) va(t)	How are things?
*Ca va!**	sa(t) va(t)	Things are fine!
Caddie	ca-D	Pull cart
Café	ca-fay	Coffee
Carotte	ca-rot	Carrot
*C'est**	say	It is...
*C'est un/une...**	say tuh/say tune	It is/this is a...
C'est de la/du...	say duh la/do	It is/this is some...
Ce sont des...	se(t) son day	It is/these are some...
*Chaise**	shayz	Chair

*Words and phrases already presented in the first book.

Charcuterie	shar-Q-terry	Delicatessen
Chat*	sha(t)	Cat
Chien*	she-N	Dog
Chocolat chaud	show-co-la show	Hot chocolate
Cinq*	sank	Five
Combien	com-B-N	How much/many?
Concombre	con-combra	Cucumber
Confiture	con-fee-tewr	Jam
Crabe	crabe	Crab
Crémerie	cray-merry	Dairy shop
Crevette	cre-vet	Shrimp
Croissant	craw-cen(t)	French roll

D

Déjeuner	day-juh-nay	Lunch
Des	day	Some
Désolé*	day-so-lay	Sorry
Dessert	day-ser	Dessert
Deux*	duh	Two
Dimanche	D-mansh	Sunday
Dîner	D-nay	Dinner
Dix*	dees	Ten
Dix-sept	dee-set	Seventeen
Dix-huit	deez-wheat	Eighteen
Dix-neuf	deez-nuhf	Nineteen
Douze	dooz	Twelve

F

Fleur*	fluhr	Flower
Franc*	fran(k)	French Franc
Fromage	fro-maj	Cheese
Fruit	fruwe	Fruit

H

Haricot vert	ar-E-co ver	Green bean
Huit*	wheat	Eight

I

Interdite	an-ter-deet	Forbidden

J

Jambon	jam-bon	Ham
Jardin du Luxembourg	jar-din due Luke-sem-burg	Luxembourg Gardens
Jaune*	joan	Yellow
Je voudrais...	juh voo-dray	I would like...
Jus d'orange	jew dO-ranj	Orange juice

L

La*	la	The (feminine)
Lait	lay	Milk
Le*	luh	The (masculine)
Légume	lay-goom	Vegetable
Les	lay	The (plural)
Louvre	loovra	Louvre

*Words and phrases already presented in the first book.

M

*Maman**	ma(t)-ma(t)	Mom
Marchand	mar-shan	Vendor
Marché	mar-shay	Market
Marionnette	ma-ree-O-net	Puppet
Médor	may-door	Pierre's dog
*Merci**	mer-see	Thank you
*Monsieur**	me(t)-sewer	Sir

N

*Neuf**	nuhf	Nine
*Non**	no	No

O

Oeufs	yew	Eggs
*Oncle**	onkla	Uncle
Onze	ownz	Eleven
*Orange**	O-ranj	Orange
Ouaf	oof	Woof
*Oui**	we	Yes

P

*Papa**	pa(t)-pa(t)	Dad
Parce que c'est comme ça!	par-se-ke say come sa	Because, that's the way it is!
Pêche	pesh	Peach
Pelouse interdite	pe-loose an-ter-deet	Keep off the grass
Petit déjeuner	pe-T day-juh-nay	Breakfast
Petit	pe-T	Small, little
Place de la Concorde	plas duh la con-cord	A square in Paris
Poire	pwar	Pear
Poisson	pwa-son	Fish
Poissonnerie	pwa-so-nerry	Fish store
Pomme	pom	Apple
Poney	po-nee	Pony
Poulet	poo-lay	Chicken
Pourpre	pour-pra	Purple
Pourquoi	pour-quaw	Why?
Prune	prune	Plum

Q

*Quatre**	catra	Four
Quatorze	ca-torz	Fourteen
*Qu'est-ce que c'est?**	kess ca(t) say	What is it?
Quinze	canz	Fifteen

R

Raisin	ray-zan	Grape
*Rouge**	rooj	Red

*Words and phrases already presented in the first book.

S

Saucisse	saw-cease	Sausage
*Sept**	set	Seven
Seize	sez	Sixteen
*S'il vous plaît**	seal-voo-play	Please
*Six**	ceese	Six

T

*Table**	ta(p)-bla	Table
*Tante**	tant	Aunt
Tomate	toe-mat	Tomato
*Tour Eiffel**	tour ay-fell	Eiffel Tower
Treize	trez	Thirteen
*Trois**	trwa	Three

U

*Un**	uh	One/A (masculine)
*Une**	(j)une	One/A (feminine)

V

*Vert**	ver	Green
Vingt	van	Twenty
Viande	V-and	Meat
Voilà	vwa-la	Here is...

All inquiries should be addressed to:
Barron's Educational Series, Inc.
250 Wireless Boulevard
Hauppauge, NY 11788

International Standard Book No. 0-8120-6384-8 (hardcover)
0-8120-1390-5 (paperback)

Library of Congress Catalog Card No. 94-26792

Library of Congress Cataloging-in-Publication Data
Bovaird, Anne Elizabeth.
    Goodbye USA, bonjour la France, II / Anne Elizabeth Bovaird ;
illustrated by Pierre Ballouhey.
        p.   cm.—(A Language learning adventure)
    English and French.
    Summary: Tom enjoys his stay in Paris and learns new French words with the help
of his cousin, aunt, and uncle. Pronunciation information is included in the text.
    ISBN 0-8120-6384-8.—ISBN 0-8120-1390-5 (pbk.)
    [1. French language—Fiction. 2. France—Fiction. 3. Cousins—Fiction.]
I. Ballouhey, Pierre, ill. II. Title. III. Series.
PC2129.E5B635   1994
[Fic]—dc20
                                                                94-26792
                                                                CIP
                                                                AC

PRINTED IN HONG KONG
4567   9955   987654321